Defeat Manipulation 101

The Secret Handbook to Defend Yourself Against Those Who Attempt to Manipulate You

By H.T. Wyatt

I0414236

Table of Contents

Introduction

You probably already know that manipulation is unethical and unpleasant. If you have been on the receiving end of manipulation, you know how badly it hurts. But the tricky thing about manipulation is that it is often subtle. You may not even realize that you are being manipulated. Alternatively, you may know that you are being manipulated, but you have no idea how to escape the control and emotionally toxic tactics of the person manipulating you.

This book is your secret weapon against manipulators. You no longer have to tolerate being manipulated. With the secrets contained in this guide, you can shake off your manipulator's control and prevent future manipulation.

This is your life. You do not need or deserve to be controlled and used by other people at their convenience. You have the right to put a stop to manipulation and take control of your life as you see fit. You are not a bad person for saying no and declaring your rights.

All human beings have certain inherent rights that we are born with. Manipulation violates all of these rights. Therefore, it is perfectly acceptable to put an end to manipulation and stand up for your human rights. You are taking your first step toward a better life free of manipulation just by picking up this guide.

When you begin to regain control of your life from manipulators, you will find that life becomes much better. You no longer feel powerless. You no longer have to do things you do not want to do. You no longer feel sucked dry of energy and resources as manipulators take everything they want from you. Empowered and strong, you will feel much happier.

Shaking off the control of manipulators is rarely easy, however. Manipulators are sneaky and often good at their craft. You may not realize you are being wronged because you have been manipulated into believing that you are somehow at fault. Well, none of that is true. No matter how difficult it is, you need to kick manipulators and their hurtful behavior right out of your life. This guide can help you understand subtle and surefire tactics that will enable you to shake off manipulation attempts.

To start, let's go over what manipulation entails. A clear grasp of all that manipulation includes can help you identify ways that you are being manipulated without even realizing it.

The word "manipulate" basically means to use a tool or piece of equipment. This definition perfectly illustrates how manipulators treat their victims. Basically, when you are being manipulated, you are being used. Manipulation is a form of mind control where manipulators get you to give them what they want. Manipulators are masters at gaining control of your mind and using you as a tool to their own ends. When they are done with you, they often throw you to the side and express no gratitude.

Manipulation is commonly defined as the use of unclear agendas in an effort to get someone to do what you want. Therefore, if you are being manipulated, you are being controlled by someone in ways that you are unaware of, for some type of end that you also do not understand. You do not have enough information about a relationship to give your consent because everything is kept murky. The relationship is not what you think it is; the things that your manipulator says to you do not necessarily have the intentions behind them that you think they do.

Manipulation requires subtlety. People hate being manipulated and will thwart it if they can tell what is going on. Therefore, manipulators are often sneaky and hard to catch in the act. They are adept at picking out people with weaknesses that they can exploit easily and successfully. When you do finally confront a manipulator, they often are able to twist the situation around and make it seem like you are somehow the one in the wrong. They will do anything to avoid getting caught in the act.

Nevertheless, manipulative people can be stopped. You only feel like you are at their mercy because they have learned how to exploit your weaknesses. They are not able to tear down your strengths. You are only giving them power over you. By taking power back for yourself, you can cripple manipulators. You will be surprised how the biggest and most harmful presences in your life are really just like scared, sneaky children when their manipulative tactics have been stripped away. These people will no longer have power over you and they will likely slink away in

shame that their attempts have been foiled.

Chapter 1: How Manipulation Can Hurt You and Why You Need to End It

It is obvious that manipulation hurts. You are being used by someone and getting nothing in return. Someone is exploiting your weaknesses and playing with your mind to get you to do things you normally would not do. Your pride and your power are being taken away by someone.

Manipulation is something that all of us do from time to time. It can be necessary for survival in some situations. You do not necessarily suffer horribly from some subtle manipulation now and then. Sometimes, you may even engage in manipulation yourself to get what you want. Ending relationships over slight manipulation is not necessary, though you have every right to put an end to any future manipulation by establishing boundaries.

But frequent manipulation poses a problem. People who are always manipulating you do not care about you and are determined to serve only their own needs. Their manipulative behavior is detrimental to your emotional well-being. The relationships that you have with manipulative people are not real relationships, but rather shams that the manipulators create to gain control over you and use of what you have to offer. These relationships will only hurt you in the long run. You do not have to tolerate them.

Manipulation and manipulative people can take a serious toll on your life. The harm caused by manipulation can manifest in many different areas of your life. As the manipulation goes on, the symptoms worsen. Manipulation makes you feel horrible, act in ways that are not normal to you, and do things that you do not want to do. It can also make you feel like you are going crazy.

Watch a reality show such as "Real Housewives" to get a sense of the trouble that manipulators cause. Nearly all of the characters are adept at manipulation. Watch how they spread rumors. Watch how they admit to the camera that they have conversations with the aim of "getting so-and-so to come around" or "getting so-and-so to do such-and-such." Yet when they have the conversation with so-and-so, they usually spin their words to hide their ultimate aim. They often do not even explore the actual topic that they are attempting to cover. After all their manipulative behavior, these women cause a lot of drama and hurt.

This is how manipulators work in your life. You are never really able to have a say in anything because you do not understand what is really going on. This is how manipulators can gain control over you and yank your life in directions that are not of your choosing. Through subliminal methods, manipulators can very quickly turn your life into a total mess. They stir up drama with others, they make you feel terrible, and they change who you are by making you set aside your true values.

Manipulators are very hurtful. They are excellent at making you doubt yourself. They also are able to use other emotions, such as guilt and

shame, to get you under their control.
Manipulators understand that by attacking your
emotional weak spots, they are able to gain the
best control over you. Unfortunately, this means
that your emotions are constantly being stirred
up and hurt. Someone is taking control of your
emotions and hurting you without your consent.

You find that you do things you do not
want to do. This can make you feel ashamed of
yourself or doubtful of your goodness as a
person. You will probably also feel guilty for how
you feel and think. You may even feel ashamed of
who you are as a person, because someone has
made you feel that you are flawed and not
worthy of being alive. All of these feelings are the
symptoms of manipulation that you must cope
with. Someone is causing you all of this pain, just

to get something that they want and are too cowardly to just ask for it! What a horrible feeling, to think that you are being used by someone who does not even care about how you feel. You are being drained for all you got by someone that is totally ungrateful and unkind.

The worst part is, manipulators rarely stick around for long. They will drop you easily and quickly when they begin to think that they can no longer use you for anything. You never mattered to them as a human, so they do not care about having you in their lives anymore unless you are adding some type of value. Therefore, manipulators will throw you away when they are done with you. You will be harmed and then you will not get a thank you or an apology.

It is time to stop this. You are a human being, not a disposable tool to be used and damaged and then thrown away. It is time to assert your humanity and demand your human rights. You no longer need to live in pain just because someone is having their way with you, throwing you around emotionally in order to gain some small goal or objective that you are not even aware of.

If you are in a manipulative romantic relationship, you may find yourself in utter misery. You doubt yourself and your sanity. You feel terrible all the time. Your partner slowly begins to tear you away from your family and friends. You give up the values you hold for your partner's, as your partner infiltrates your mind and your life. Suddenly, you may find yourself a completely different person. You are in a situation that utterly hurts you and was not what you signed up for. In addition, you may wake up one day and find that the person that you gave everything to has dumped you. Now, you are totally alone.

It is time to reclaim your sanity. End a manipulative relationship before it gets to a desperate point. This will not end well, so you need to end it now.

Unfortunately, it can be hard to want to leave a manipulator. They are great at being charming or playing the victim; basically, they can show any face that they need to show to get you to stick around. In addition, they may make you feel that if you leave, you will be alone forever, because who else could put up with you?

Ignore the faces and words a manipulator uses when you try to leave, and instead focus on their behavior. Their actions hurt you, so why tolerate it anymore? You can find someone better, regardless of how your partner makes you feel.

Family can also be manipulative. Many people grow up with a manipulative mother or father or both. Manipulative siblings may be problematic, too, as they develop manipulation skills to get attention and win at sibling rivalry over the years. Manipulative family members can scar you. You grow up with low self-esteem. You feel ashamed of who you are and guilty for how you feel. You never speak up, for fear of being torn down. The manipulative relationships that you grew up around also set the standard for your future relationships. You are more likely to choose manipulative and emotionally abusive partners if you are used to being treated that way. Your low self-esteem is a weakness that manipulators can smell from miles away and will be eager to exploit.

Setting boundaries with family is essential here. You need to follow the tips in this book to make your family relationships bearable. Sometimes, distance from family members is necessary. However, this does not mean that you cannot talk to family members just because they are manipulative. You can halt the abuse and manipulation.

The worst manipulators can be found at work. These are people that you cannot just escape from. They make you feel horrible and get you to overwork or do jobs that are not yours to do. They get you to compromise your emotions. They spread hurtful rumors and tell humiliating jokes about you to the rest of the staff.

Again, you must use the tips in this book to protect yourself from work manipulators. These are not necessarily people that you can just avoid or run away from. You must work with them every day. But unfortunately, this means that it is harder to protect yourself. These tips can help you set boundaries and make manipulators shrink away from you as they realize their antics will not fly with you.

Chapter 2: How to Spot a Manipulator

Anyone can be a master manipulator. Manipulators are not necessarily people in positions of power or scary-looking people with obvious cards up their sleeves. In fact, they are usually more innocent, powerless, and unattractive people who must use manipulation tactics to get their way because they cannot in other ways.

People often learn manipulation skills as survival tactics when they are young. It may be the only way that they can deal with abusive parents or get their way in a household full of siblings that they are in constant competition with. However, their manipulation skills became habits as they reached adulthood, and now it is part of who they are.

Since you cannot spot a manipulator just by appearance, you must gauge someone's manipulative qualities based on how they treat you and how they make you feel. There are many little signs that can indicate an underlying manipulative relationship that is not healthy. Even if your interactions with someone seem normal on the surface, your internal feelings can show you the truth.

The main thing you need to watch for is how you feel when you leave a situation with someone. If you walk away from an exchange with someone feeling awful, you may have just been emotionally manipulated.

People who make you feel horrible about yourself or make you feel constantly guilty are manipulating you with guilt. They are making you feel like you are always at fault. You really are not at fault. Rather, these people are wronging you and making you feel that you are the one who is wronging them in order for them to escape consequences. We all make mistakes, but no one is ever at fault for everything, all the time. People who constantly make you feel guilty or lay blame on you are not telling the truth. Rather, they are manipulating you and it is time to put an end to it!

Another sign that you are being manipulated is when you begin to doubt yourself and your own sanity. You may be the victim of gaslighting or pathological lying if someone makes you feel like you are somehow crazy. These are especially problems in families or romantic relationships, where a manipulator spends a lot of time around you and is able to undermine your sanity.

Gaslighting refers to when a person tells you that you are crazy and the obvious is not true. For instance, if you think that the lights are dimmer in your house and the manipulator turned them down, he or she may lie and say that the lights are normal and you are just imagining things. Gaslighting is scary because it can erase your confidence and certainty in life. It gives the manipulator the ultimate control in deciding how you perceive reality.

Pathological lying is just as harmful as gaslighting. A persistent and frequent liar will make you doubt yourself and what is real. You will never quite know if he or she is telling the truth – or if it is just another lie. As your trust fades, so does your certainty.

If there is someone in your life that you are scared of confronting or talking to about things, you may be encountering a manipulator as well. People who tell you that what you think, feel, or need is wrong are manipulating you. As a human being, you have the right to demand that your needs be met. Being told that you are wrong all the time violates this right. You begin to live in fear of your manipulator because you know that anything you ask for will be denied and you will be made to feel guilty or wrong somehow for your most basic feelings.

This includes people who tell hurtful jokes, then tell you to get over your hurt because it was funny. These people are doing something wrong and they are refusing to acknowledge that what they said was not OK. They try to manipulate you into thinking that you are somehow wrong for taking a joke too seriously.

People who predict doom onto you are sometimes trying to manipulate you. Family is especially good at discouraging you from doing what you want by saying that something horrible will happen or you will fail. They may also try to keep you down so that they can control you. Manipulators will predict things like, "You could never do a job like that" or "You will be a horrible mother!"

In addition, there are people who will say anything to get you to do what they want. They may do things to annoy you. Or they may say upsetting things. Their ultimate aim is to get you to break down and say yes just to get rid of them. Excessively annoying people and people who drain your energy may be manipulators. You never want to leave a social interaction feeling exhausted and unhappy. Feeling this way is a sign of something troubling going on under the surface.

A good way to tell if you are being manipulated is if someone does something bad to you. Yet when you confront him or her, suddenly it becomes all about you. "You were the one who was being mean! You deserved what you got!" These are all lies that good manipulators will tell you to distract you from the fact that they just did something wrong. Manipulators will do anything to avoid facing consequences for their actions, and one of their best tactics is to make you feel like it is all your fault.

Another sign that you are being manipulated is when you have resolves, values, or boundaries that you stand by, then suddenly find yourself discarding these for a person. Someone asks you to do something that you are not comfortable with and you do it. You find yourself in situations and performing actions that go against who you are. This means that someone is good at convincing you to neglect yourself to get what they want.

You cannot always spot a manipulator right off the bat. It takes some time and some observation to realize who in your life has an ulterior motive. However, here are some behaviors in others that you should watch out for. They are hints of manipulative personalities or hidden intents.

Excessive flattery is usually a bad sign. Manipulators will use excessive flattery to get you to feel wonderful so that you do anything they want. A compliment here and there is great, but someone who constantly compliments you is exhibiting some alarming behavior. Often the office or class kiss-ass is a manipulator who uses flattery to get the boss or teacher to favor him. A romantic partner that overwhelms you with gifts, kisses, and romantic calls are likely attempting to seduce you so that you ignore more troubling signs.

Pushy people are also possible manipulators. Think of pushy salespeople who will not take no for an answer. Manipulators are using the same tactic, and pushing on you till you give in just to get them to go away. They act overbearing until you cannot say no any longer. Salespeople often employ manipulation tactics so watch for salesperson-like behavior in those around you. Your loved ones should not be acting like they are trying to close a deal with you all the time.

Gossiping is another bad sign. Someone who talks badly about everyone else in the office is most likely trying to get you to feel comfortable enough to say something bad about others yourself. Then, the gossip will go on to repeat what you said to everyone else. Gossips thrive on creating drama and are often skilled at getting the information from others that they can use to stir the pot. They are also capable of starting rumors that are based on nothing. Often, gossips are talking just as badly about you behind your back as they talk to you about everyone else. Never trust a gossip and be wary of their manipulative troublemaking behavior.

Frequent lying is a sign that someone has no respect for you as a person and is willing to say anything to get certain reactions from you. It is a bad sign in any person, but can be a troubling sign of a manipulative personality. Lying and manipulating are both forms of deception and so they often go hand-in-hand.

Above all, learn to rely on your gut. You can sense when someone is not being honest with you. Do you ever get the feeling that someone is lying to you, or that they do not want to help you with something even though they volunteered their assistance? You are sensing their manipulation at play. Your gut is always right. If you feel something is off about a person, then it most likely is.

Chapter 3: Manipulation Tactics You Need to Watch for

The art of manipulation is relatively simple, despite its complicated effects on people. Manipulation works by either offering you a valuable gain or a horrible loss. A manipulator puts him- or herself in a position of power by gaining insight into what you want and what you fear, and then using those things against you.

The following are tactics that manipulators commonly use:

Making an Offer You Can't Refuse

Manipulators are great at reading people. They can tell what you want and then promise it to you to get you under their spell. A manipulator will figure out just how to approach you. They might use seduction to feed your ego if you are vain. They might play the victim and make you feel sorry for them if you are a protective and providing type. They might offer you security if you are in an insecure place in life.

Be careful when someone seems perfect and offers you great things. Manipulators are everywhere and they often come in shiny packages. You do not need to rely on someone to get the things you want, so don't fall into the trap that manipulators lay out for you. The things you want should not be bait.

Exploiting Your Fear

Manipulators will find the source of your deepest fears, and then threaten you with what you fear the most. Most people want to be loved and fear not being loved. The most insecure people are unable to live alone, and therefore require someone to love them. Manipulators will use the threat of withdrawing their love as a way to get you to do what they want. "I will break up with you if you don't come to this party," is an example of how manipulators will use love and fear as a means to get their way. Often, manipulators will employ the silent treatment, which is just another form of love withdrawal.

Loving yourself can help you gain immunity to this tactic. Stop depending on manipulators for their fake form of love. It is better to be alone and without them than playing their games. No one who really loves you will be able to drop you out of their life or stop talking to you for days just because you didn't do exactly what they wanted.

Blackmail

You made the mistake of telling a manipulator something personal. Now, they hang it over your head every day. They make you live in fear and do what they want just so that they do not share the information they have on you.

This is not the CIA or a crime show. Blackmail is not supposed to be a part of daily life. If someone is blackmailing you, you should not tolerate it. Consider how badly it would hurt you if the truth got out. Maybe it would not be so bad. You need to stop fearing the manipulator.

Passive-Aggressive Behavior

Nothing is ever straightforward when you are dealing with a manipulator. For instance, a manipulative roommate might ask you to take out the trash. Instead of just saying, "Please take out the trash," the roommate will leave a note on the fridge that says, "Hey guys! I have taken out the trash many times this week and I am exhausted from work. It would be nice if I didn't have to do it every time. Thanks!" Manipulators use passive-aggressiveness to constantly attack you for what you are supposedly doing wrong, without ever phrasing their confrontations in a way that you can call them out on. They avoid being openly aggressive so that you cannot say they are doing anything wrong. "I asked nicely," is how they defend passive-aggression.

Well, no. They did not ask nicely. Passive-aggressive behavior is just as harmful as aggressive behavior. In fact, it may be worse, because the manipulator is being sneaky and covert while being rude. Call people out on this type of behavior and do not let them say that they asked nicely. You have a right to demand that the passive-aggressive nonsense ends.

Gossiping

Instead of confronting you about something directly, manipulators will do it in a roundabout way. They might smile at you and say that everything is great, then tell everyone else in the office how horrible you are. That way, they can ensure that you will hear the news of how unhappy they are, but not from them. They can avoid any kind of confrontation with you and pass the responsibility of working things out with you onto other people.

This is just cowardly. It is best to approach a manipulator directly when you hear rumors of how unhappy they are with you. Force your manipulator to talk to you directly.

Changing the Energy of a Room

Manipulators have an eerie ability to change the vibe of a room. If a manipulator is upset, he or she will pout and do everything possible to bring the mood of a room down. People will get so fed up that they will do anything just to get the manipulator to stop ruining a party or get-together with negative vibes. If a manipulator does not want to be somewhere, they will let you know!

Really, this tactic is silly. Manipulators are acting like small children, pouting to get what they want. But their moodiness can really put people off and can drag you down. It is best to avoid these party-poopers as they are just childish losers who are selfish enough to ruin something for everybody to get one thing.

Causing Drama

Just like manipulators will lower the vibe of a room just to get people to give in to their demands, they will also go out of their way to create unbearable situations designed to make people cave. Manipulators will throw tantrums and create drama and say humiliating things until you finally can't stand it anymore and give in to what they want, just to get them to back off. For instance, perhaps someone does not want to go with you to a party, but you ask them to. So they come along and spend the whole time embarrassing you or fighting, until you get so embarrassed that you say, "Let's just leave."

You do not need to tolerate this childish behavior. Tantrums and games are not permitted in your life anymore. You need to tell manipulators to knock it off or else invite them to leave a situation that they are trying to ruin. Do not ever give into what they want, or they will keep acting this way.

Lying

Manipulators are not direct people. Therefore, it makes sense that they are often pathological liars. They use lies to avoid confrontation with you, to hide their interior motives, and finally to make you question your sanity. You might hear a manipulator say something and when you confront them about it later, they will smile and lie that you must have misheard because they most definitely did not say that. You can't prove what they said, so you are left wondering if you really did mishear or if they are lying. Lying removes trust from a relationship and keeps you in a position of constant wondering and confusion.

Liars are best to be avoided. Liars are harmful people with no respect for your wishes or your need for honesty. A little dishonesty is common in any relationship, but frequent lying is grounds for ending a relationship. You would be foolish to keep trusting the person and

thinking that they will stop lying out of love for
you.

Positive Reinforcement

Manipulators are great at letting you win
sometimes. This is positive reinforcement. It
works by disguising the fact that your
manipulator is really the one gaining everything
in this relationship. Manipulators will let you
think that you are winning in more unimportant
cases so that they can have an edge when they
really need it. "I let you win last time. Why can't I
win this time? Just this one time?"

The people who give in the most are often
manipulators. They are just playing you. Be wary
of passive and non-confrontational people who

always agree with you and give in to you. They may have a trick or two up their sleeve.

Keeping the Spotlight on Them

You have a headache and your manipulator has brain cancer. Manipulators are inherently selfish people who have no respect for you. If you confide in them that you are suffering or struggling, they will discount your suffering and make you feel guilty for even complaining by turning the spotlight onto themselves. Whatever bad is happening to you, they will claim that they are dealing with much worse.

This is just a tactic to take away your right to feel and express your needs. If someone dominates conversations and dismisses everything you say, this person has no respect for you. You should move on to someone who actually listens and cares.

Blaming You

Nothing is ever the manipulator's fault. Meanwhile, you get blamed for literally everything. You will hear more about what you do wrong than what you do right. This tactic is designed to strip away your self-esteem and make you feel like you are a terrible person. A manipulator thinks that if you believe you are responsible for everything wrong, you will not notice how the manipulator is doing you wrong. You will just blame yourself for everything that is happening, and you will not blame them for anything. A web of guilt is now cast around you and you are paralyzed from taking action.

But no one is perfect. No one is utterly bad, either. You are not at fault for everything. If someone blames you a lot, you should look at what they do wrong. They are probably not saints.

Playing the Victim

Manipulators find that playing the victim allows them to act as if they are doing nothing wrong. By playing the victim, they hope to garner everyone's sympathy. That way, people excuse their manipulative actions and do not have the heart to say no or call manipulators out on bad behavior.

For example, if you tell someone who is manipulative that you are upset that she forgot your birthday, she will come back with, "I am so sorry I forgot your birthday! I just have so much pain in my life right now because of my break up and all that has been going on. I'm so sorry that I didn't put my feelings aside and focus on the fact that it was your birthday! Your birthday is way more important!" By doing this, the manipulator places herself in a victim position, while making you feel like you did something wrong to her by expecting that she remember your birthday.

Do not buy into this game. No one is ever the victim all of the time. If you confront someone and they try to distract you by making you feel sorry for them, then you can just say, "I'm sorry, but that is no excuse for how you are acting."

Chapter 4: Why You?

You may wonder what you are doing wrong to attract so many bad people into your life. You figure that you must give out some vibe that acts like a sign on your forehead declaring, "Use me! I'm a sucker!"

There is nothing wrong with you. None of this is your fault. But understanding the traits that make you an ideal victim for manipulators can help you begin to overcome those traits as you learn to combat manipulation, which we cover in the next chapter.

Being an Empath

Being an empath does not mean that you are empathetic. Most people possess empathy.

Empaths, instead, are very special people who are especially sensitive and attuned to the vibes of the world around them. This makes them able to sense things that others would never guess. They possess excellent people-reading skills because they feel others' emotions and vibes.

You may wonder how you can fall into the traps of so many manipulators if you are an empath and have such great people-reading skills. You can tell a million things about a person just by glancing at them, yet you can't seem to tell when someone in your life is bad for you. You are always right about your friend's dates, but never about your own. You keep picking bad people to be your lovers and your friends, despite your excellent discernment of others' choices in lovers and friends. This is because you are too nice. And you are too nice because you are an empath.

Unfortunately, it is also true that empaths feel the suffering of the world around them as their own pain. In an effort to relieve this pain, they try to help the world out by being kind. Sometimes they are kind to the wrong people. They let manipulators in by being obliging and then they are too nice to kick them out. Manipulators love to feed on empaths, because empaths are likely to say yes to them and give them what they want in an effort to "just be nice."

Fortunately for you, being an empath means that you are also naturally equipped with the best manipulator-sensors around. If you begin to learn the signs of manipulations and manipulative people, you can begin to very easily and accurately pinpoint people who have bad intentions for you. You are already adept at reading people because you are so sensitive naturally. The power to spot and stop manipulators already lies within you. Stop ignoring your gut just to be nice, and instead be firm against manipulators. The bad vibes you get off of people are very real and very helpful in improving the quality of people that you interact with.

Being Insecure

If you have a large amount of self-doubt and low self-esteem, you are a magnet for manipulators. Manipulators will love to feed on you because you do not have the self-respect to tell them off, and you have blatant insecurities that they can feed off of.

Your insecurities usually reflect things that you are afraid of. If you are insecure, most likely your deepest fear is not being loved or lovable. As you seek affirmation that you are lovable, you play right into the hands of manipulators who offer you the feeling of being loved as they exploit you. In addition, manipulators can trap you with fear by planting the idea into your head that no one else can love you. Because of your insecurities, you believe them. Hence, you remain in the relationship because you think that it is your only hope.

Showing your insecurities is almost a petty way of getting positive reinforcement. You beg for love and as a result, you often get manipulated. Rather, it is better to work on loving yourself. There is no one else on earth like you. So why hate yourself? You are loved and lovable. You need to realize this fact, and begin to believe it wholeheartedly. Stop letting people hurt you because you deserve so much better. With confidence and self-esteem in your heart, you are less of a magnet for manipulators. They will not see any fears and doubts in you that they can easily exploit.

Being Vulnerable

What you fear the most and what you want the most are two things that manipulators seek to know about you. By knowing these two things about you, manipulators are able to hook into you by playing on what you want the most and by threatening you with what you fear the most. These two vital pieces of information about yourself are what make you vulnerable. They are, in essence, your "hooks" that pull in manipulators and bad people who just want to use you.

It is easy to be in a vulnerable place in your life where you really want something. Maybe you desire security and comfort in a relationship. Maybe you want sexual fulfillment and fun. Whatever you desire from other people, it is not wrong to have wants and needs. However, manipulators will see your needs and try to use them to their own advantage. A manipulator will think, "What can I offer her so that she will think that she needs to be with me?"

After hooking you with a promise of something that you want, a manipulator will then exploit your greatest fears. If you fear growing old, they will tell you that you are already showing signs of aging. They will say anything to make you scared and to make you rely on them for some type of protection. They will make you feel like you have no alternative options and no hope.

By enticing you with what you want and then threatening you with what you fear, manipulators can spin a tight spider web of emotions around you. Soon, you become dependent on them to shield you from your fear and give you what you want.

Basically, anyone is vulnerable to manipulation. And, really, almost everyone is vulnerable to some degree. All of us, or at least almost all of us, have fallen into the trap of manipulation at least once in our lives. But what can make you especially vulnerable is when you have easily exploitable wants and fears. Some of the most vulnerable people are people who are addicted to drugs, who are single parents, or who need something desperately, such as affection or even just a place to stay. Having a very visible want and a very obvious fear can make you easily available and very attractive to manipulators.

Being vulnerable does not mean that you can't have fears or wants. These things make you human. You just have to learn to protect yourself. Do not put your fears and your desires out on public display. Watch who you talk to, because not everyone who smiles at you is your friend. The best listeners and nicest co-workers may just be reading you to see if you will be a great victim. Recognize when someone is trying to use you, and put an end to the interaction. Also, be more discerning of those who try to appeal to your needs. Do not take people up on tempting offers of what you want just because they offer. This is especially true if you are seeking love and someone approaches you, offering affection. Instead, carefully get to know people, and make sure that they are not just trying to manipulate you for some end.

Periods of Your Life that Make You Vulnerable

It is not always some inherent trait within you that makes you susceptible to manipulation. You may be in a phase of your life that is making you more vulnerable. There are many phases in life where you become more emotionally vulnerable and unable to defend yourself. Typically, these periods involve transition. Transition is never easy or comfortable. As you make a transition, you are heading into unknown territory. It is normal to be scared and to emit a need for another person to lean on. Sadly, this need can set you up to look like a perfect victim.

Transition is when you are affecting a big change in your life or a change has happened to you against your will. It can include when you are trying to change yourself, but you are rife with doubts because you do not know what you are really doing in life yet or if you have made a good choice. Manipulators will dive in when you are unsure of yourself. They will pretend to have all the answers that you are looking for and also a shoulder for you to cry on.

A transitional period of life can also include when you make a big life change, such as a move or a career switch. Your doubt and uncertainty, and your possible loneliness and disorientation in your new environment, make you send out the signal that you need some type of support. Manipulators will be right there, pretending to be your friend while secretly driving their own motive.

A transitional period can also include when something bad has happened to you. Perhaps you just got dumped. Perhaps you just lost someone close to you. Being in a period of emotional vulnerability can place you in a situation where your fears and needs are naked. Manipulators are likely to spot you in your ugly situation, and they swoop in, knowing that you need something. Whether you need a hug or a shoulder to cry on, your pain is evident and manipulators are ready to use it to their own advantage.

If you are existing in a period of instability, you may not be able to care for yourself. You may need shelter, food, money, or other basic needs for survival. You are also living under a lot of stress and are emotionally wounded as a result. Therefore, you are in a very vulnerable position where you must rely on others. Manipulators will take advantage of your period of severe need by giving you what you need the most, but never for free. Watch out for overly generous people and kind hearts. While there are kind people in the world, people who offer to help you out in times of need while asking nothing in exchange are potentially manipulators staking their claim on you as their newest victim. It is not unusual for homeless children to be taken into homes and then molested, for instance. Most kindness carries with it a price.

Chapter 5: How to Combat Manipulation

Manipulators only gain control over their victims because they are able to weave webs of emotions around their victims, thus trapping their victims in fear and co-dependency. Really, they do not have as much power over others as they seem to have. Usually, they are harmful people, but only because their victims give them the power to be harmful. Without being given control, manipulators are often pathetic people that have basically nothing going for them but their clever manipulation skills. They may be charming and they may be manipulative, but beneath their facades, they are powerless jokes. Often they are lonely people, with little love in their lives. They hate themselves and they are always unhappy.

You may be afraid of the manipulators in your life. The fear can be very extreme because of the tight emotional control that manipulators have gained over your mind. But when you start to look at these people from an outside perspective, you will be shocked at what losers they really are. They probably have much less to give to the world than you do, despite what they tell you. They also do not have much in the way of good heartedness, since they are selfish users who are out to hurt you just to satisfy their own needs. Probably they have few true friends and no self-love. It is likely that your manipulative partner provides you with very little in reality, and your manipulative family members or co-workers are not excelling at life as much as they want to believe that they are.

You will find it hilarious when you start to realize how low and silly the manipulators in your life are. Then, you will start to take them less seriously. Without fear clouding your judgment, you can begin to combat manipulation and take down manipulators in your life.

Manipulation is horrible. You may feel that you have no way out. But you are not trapped. There are ways to defeat manipulation so that you can live a happier life surrounded by genuine people.

Demand Your Human Rights

The first step to combatting manipulation is to understand your basic human rights. These are rights that all people have without question. Laws of ethics in psychology, for instance, treat these basic human rights as the foundations of their philosophy. You should too.

As a human being, you have these rights and you should not let anyone deny them to you. Unfortunately, when you are being manipulated, you are having your basic human rights violated. It is time to put an end to that. You deserve to be treated with respect and to have your rights acknowledged by those around you. It is time for you to begin asking people to treat you with your rights in mind.

If people cannot honor your rights, then you have every right to offer them consequences for treating you badly. You also have every right to limit contact with people who cannot honor your human rights.

Your basic human rights include:

- **The right to being treated with respect**

    You have the right to be treated with respect. How you define "respect" is really up to you. But the way that you want to be treated is how you should be treated. People should speak to you without trying to hurt your feelings. They should avoid deliberately mentioning things that hurt you or tear you down or talking to you in a demeaning manner. Name calling, eye rolling, yelling, snapping, and sarcasm are all rude mannerisms that are very disrespectful.

- **The right to express thoughts, feelings, and needs**

You are human and you have needs, feelings, and thoughts. You should not have to live as if in a closet, with all of your feelings and thoughts shut away. Being vocal about who you are without fear or shame is one of your basic human rights. People who make you feel bad about expressing yourself are not good for you. Whether they make you feel guilty for demanding respect or they make you feel like

you are not good enough, they have
no right to offer you negative
consequences for expressing
yourself.

- **The right to set your own
  priorities**

  Your life is yours to live. You can
  set priorities and make plans for
  yourself. Only you know what is
  best for you. Therefore, you can
  make decisions based on what you
  think is best and you do not have to
  feel guilty about what others think.
  People who try to make you
  question or feel guilty for making
  your life your own are
  manipulators who are just trying to

gain control over you. Take away their control and control your own life.

- **The right to say no without feeling guilty**

  You have the right to say no if you want to. Other people may get mad, but that is their problem, not yours. You should never feel guilty for saying no. If someone is adept at making you say yes to avoid feeling guilty, you are dealing with classic manipulation. Never put your own needs aside to accommodate someone else's. When you say no, you mean no. You have a right to take care of yourself. There is no need for guilt and worry about others' feelings.

- **The right to protect yourself**

  You have every right to defend yourself from harm. If you see a way to protect yourself, you may do so. No one else can prevent you from protecting yourself. Making you feel like you are somehow bad for protecting yourself is just manipulation. Ignore it.

- **The right to create your own life without the control and approval of others**

  As an adult, you do not need permission to live your life. You can make your own decisions without the approval or control of others. If someone is always trying to run your life, he or she is an over controlling manipulator. Even if this person is your parent, they are being overly controlling and you have the right to live your own life now that you are an adult. You need to set boundaries and stand up for what you believe in and what choices you have made. You do not need to live worrying about whether or not someone will approve.

Avoid Manipulative People When Possible

Obviously, you need to stay away from manipulative people. This is not always easy, but it is best. Say good-bye to bad people in your life. If someone brings down your mood or exhibits any of the behaviors we talked about earlier, you need to put an end to the unhealthy relationship.

There is really no other way to completely defeat manipulation. Manipulators will not tolerate confrontation well. If you confront them, they will twist it around on you and make you seem like the one in the wrong. If you try to reason with them, they will hit you with irrational claims and then emotional tricks to get you to question your senses and ability to reason. Nothing works one hundred percent of the time besides leaving manipulators behind and moving on with your life.

Manipulators are doing something terrible. Emotional manipulation is truly awful and dangerous to your overall emotional health. You do not need to feel horrible about kicking manipulators out of your life. The pain they express when you kick them out is not real pain, but rather desperation to get you back. Don't fall for it. Just move on.

Remove Your Fear of Withdrawal of Love

Many manipulators will use the threat of withdrawing their love to make you do what they want. People usually want to be loved and this desire can create a weakness that manipulators can exploit.

You can protect yourself by loving yourself. Know that you are all that you really need. You don't need someone else's love, especially when their love is contingent on you doing things for them. They clearly don't love you and your relationship is not healthy. Therefore, stop relying on that fake love and instead rely on the only love that you can guarantee: your own self-love.

When you love yourself, you no longer require the love of anyone else. That way, manipulators cannot threaten you with love withdrawal because not being loved by others no longer scares you. You know that while it feels nice to be loved, you do not need to depend on someone's conditional love to be happy. You have been alone before and it will not kill you now. In fact, it is better to be lonely and alone, than being unhappy with a manipulator who threatens to take away the love you rely on as your rock when you don't follow his or her rules.

You will become invulnerable. You will also stop caring about people who manipulate you. Your new self-respect will attract better people into your life.

Start loving yourself. Repeat to yourself throughout the day, "I love myself." Then really feel a flush of self-love. This will train your mind to actually love yourself, flaws and all. You are uniquely you, the only version of you on this planet. That makes you very special. Even with your flaws, you are lovable and wonderful and need to realize that.

Continue to Say No

Whatever you do, do not ever give in to a manipulator. The more you give in, the more you encourage the disrespectful behavior. Hold your ground and continue to say no. When you say no, it means no. No matter how much someone pleads or manipulates or guilts you, the answer is NO.

Perhaps you have a reputation as someone who gives in after being asked enough times. Stop being that person. You should stand by your words, including your dissenting words. You will gain more respect that way. Since manipulators operate on disrespect, then you will be able to eliminate them from your life.

This also includes standing by confrontations. If someone hurts you and you confront them, stand by the fact that they hurt you. Don't follow their little emotional manipulation games of how you are at fault and they had every right to hurt you. No, they hurt you, and that is all there is to it. You have the right to feel hurt, no matter what excuse your manipulator gives for hurting you. Don't let excuses make you retract your statements. If you do, then you are giving manipulators a sign that they can win again in the future.

Take Time

When asking you to do something, a manipulator often puts pressure on you to say yes immediately. By putting a sense of urgency on you, manipulators are able to limit your judgment and the amount of time you can spend analyzing something to determine if you can truly gain anything from it. Salespeople are particularly adept at forcing you into a decision by making you feel that you have to sign the deal now or you will lose this "amazing opportunity" forever.

Ask for more time before making a decision and then get away from the person so you can reasonably reach a decision on your own. Do not let pressure manipulate you into a decision when you are still unsure, or else you will regret it later. Think over the pros and cons of a purchase, or whatever someone is manipulating you into. Say, "I have to think about this" and then leave so that you can really think about it.

Urgency is a great and common manipulation tactic. But the actual urgency of a situation is rarely ever true. People force their priorities onto you but their priorities are not your priorities. One of your human rights is to set your own priorities, actually. So set them by taking the time you need to make a decision. Do not let others' sense of urgency or attempts to pressure you make you feel like something is actually urgent and you need to make a decision.

Reject Feeling Guilty or Ashamed

If you know that you are being played into a trap with guilt or shame, you can help break out of this trap by rejecting all feelings of guilt or shame when dealing with the manipulative person who likes to make you feel these ways. Decide to no longer let these emotions rule your life. There is no truth to these emotions, and you have no need to feel guilty or ashamed of yourself.

If someone starts to make you feel this way, just say, "I won't be guilted about this any longer." Or try, "I'm sorry, but I actually like myself. You can't make me feel ashamed and tear me down anymore." These words may come out brittle, but you will have just established a tremendous amount of power over your manipulator.

Stop Blaming Yourself

Manipulators are great at making you feel that you are at fault. But you do not deserve to be used and abused, no matter what you have done. Therefore, you do not deserve manipulation and you in no way bring it on yourself. Nothing a manipulator does is OK or justified.

If someone wrongs you, don't let them make you feel guilty. They should be ashamed of themselves. You have the right to stand your ground and declare that you are not in the wrong here. If they refuse to acknowledge that, that is their problem. You know in your heart when you are being manipulated. It is not OK and you are not at fault.

Call Manipulators Out

Call manipulators out on their behavior. They will react defensively and deny your claims and even try to make you seem like the manipulative one. But you will know that you are right. Just walk away when someone argues with you. You know you had a right to confront them, and really they know too. Call gossips and liars out and walk away when they argue as well; they are the ones in the wrong, so don't let them manipulate you.

When other people wrong you, it is OK to confront them, openly but diplomatically. State how they made you feel and how you do not appreciate what they did. They will most likely refuse to apologize and instead try to manipulate you more, but try to see their actions for what they are. It will become hilariously apparent how manipulative people are when they try to desperately get you to not be angry with them, when you have every right to be.

Ask Probing Questions

Manipulators are great at keeping the attention on you and what you did wrong. They will do anything to keep the spotlight on them...except when it comes to their manipulation tactics. This is because manipulators are attempting to do something covert on you because they know that they are in the wrong. When you call attention to what they are doing, they become very defensive and uncomfortable. Asking probing questions is a great way to put the heat on a manipulator and make him or her extremely uncomfortable. Nine times out of ten, your questions will make the manipulator stop what he or she is doing out of discomfort and nervousness.

When a manipulator starts to make demands on you or mess with your mind, you can turn the tables on them by asking them probing questions.

"Why are you doing this?

"What exactly do you hope to gain from telling me this sob story?"

"Do you think you are being reasonable right now?"

"Are you asking me to do something for you, or telling me?"

"What do I stand to get out of this?"

"Do I even have a say? Or am I just doing what you want to do?"

"Are you telling me the truth, one hundred percent? Are you sure?"

Manipulators won't like this one bit! Especially liars, who will become incredibly uncomfortable when put under the microscope. Asking these questions enables manipulators to see their own games and the fact that you are onto them.

Use Reverse Psychology

Reverse psychology works when you tell someone something that is opposite what you want. You can use this tactic on manipulators by basically manipulating them right back. When someone tries to manipulate you, give them the opposite reaction to what they want. This will disconcert them and show them that they are losing control.

Once you get a sense for what a manipulator wants, you can decide to give them the opposite reaction. Say a manipulator says a horrible thing about you to get you upset. React with laughter or a smile.

Or say that a manipulator repeats something your co-worker said about you in order to turn you against him. Instead of giving in and becoming angry at the co-worker, get angry at the manipulator. "What I want to know is, why did he feel comfortable saying mean things about me to you? What were you saying back? I think you are a liar and a bad friend."

If a manipulator wants something from you, give them the opposite. A manipulator who wants money from you should get a job application. A manipulator who wants you to give him a ride to the mall can get a bike or a nice pair of walking shoes instead.

Give Them a Taste of Their Own Medicine

Mirror manipulators' behavior. They will hate this. When you mirror them, they can see how nasty they really are. They will recognize their tricks in your behavior and feel guilty as they realize how badly their tricks make others feel. In addition, they will feel ashamed that you have found out their sly tricks. Manipulators will not enjoy being treated as badly as they treat others. Manipulators are people with feelings, too, and they want respect just as much as you do. But they have not earned that respect by acting cowardly and using covert, sneaky tricks to gain mind control over you. Therefore, violate their respect and teach them how it feels. They will learn a quick lesson how badly it feels to be manipulated. This will accomplish one of two things. Either they will either flee far away from you to escape your attacks, or they will feel bad when they see similarities between how you treat them and how they treat you.

Unfortunately, this is very dangerous. Often manipulators are emotionally disturbed people who are incapable of doubt, shame, or remorse. Mirroring their behavior will often have no result because disturbed people cannot feel the emotions that their tactics are meant to stir up. Mirroring works best with people in your life who are not disturbed but who suddenly want to try manipulating. For instance, your children may go through manipulative phases as they try out how to communicate with others. Mirroring their behavior can be effective. Typically, however, mirroring will accomplish nothing but harm to yourself, so it is best avoided.

In addition, if you have a conscience, you may not want to try this. Why act just like people who do not care about others' feelings? You are better than that. Mirroring is best only when you are trying to teach a valuable lesson and salvage a relationship from manipulative behavior. It should not be your go-to tactic, or then you become a manipulator yourself.

Take Notes or Record Conversations

If someone is gaslighting you by denying things that they clearly said a few minutes ago or otherwise making you question your senses, you are within your rights to start taking notes. It may be helpful to record conversations on your phone or other device, or take notes during arguments in a little notebook. Manipulators who employ gaslighting as part of their technique will positively hate this. They will probably freak out. This is because they know that you can now prove their manipulation.

It may be awkward to always record conversations. The paranoia required to do this will be annoying. But once you start, you will begin to realize that you are not insane. The other person is the one who is manipulating you into questioning your own mind. Then you will probably want to end the relationship with this manipulative person. If you have to take notes to stay sane in any kind of relationship with another person, you do not need to be in that relationship. You are not insane and you do not need to feel like you are. Insanity is very scary and unpleasant, and doubting your sanity can put you in a horrible, vulnerable place of pain and doubt and confusion. End that now.

Set Consequences

Just as a child has consequences for breaking curfew, people should also suffer consequences for manipulating you. If someone toxic wants to remain in your life, he or she must promise to respect you. When he or she fails to do this, he or she should face some consequences.

Set consequences for people who cross your boundaries. To do this, you first must set very clear boundaries. Your basic human rights listed above is a great place to start when creating reasonable boundaries that no one can cross. Your boundaries should include: No one can disrespect me. No one can control my life. No one can make me feel guilty for how I feel when I express my feelings. No one should tell me that black is white or the sky is purple. No one can lie to me.

When someone crosses your boundaries, hold them accountable. Do not let their excuses and little guilt games get to you. Tell them how badly they made you feel and then tell them that they cannot do this again. Then offer them a consequence. It could be ignoring them, it could be cutting off money that you are giving them, it could be refusing to do them a favor. By cutting manipulators off, you are no longer allowing yourself to be used, and you are teaching manipulators that they cannot get what they want by messing with your mind.

Most importantly, stand by what you say. If you offer a consequence to a manipulator, follow through with it. For instance, if a family member asks for money but then tries to guilt you into giving it, you can say, "I would give you money, but you just tried guilting me. I don't like that. So I think it's best you seek a loan elsewhere." Then continue to refuse to give a loan, no matter how desperately the manipulator attempts to get you to change your mind. Manipulators may use sweet talk or guilt or rage to talk you into something, but you need to stand by your no. This can make manipulators learn respect for you and can end their toxic behavior.

You don't need someone else's validation for this. People may not agree with giving your loved ones consequences of any kind. It doesn't matter. You need to do something to end manipulation, no matter how mean it may seem to others. Others are not in your shoes so their judgment is neither helpful nor acceptable.

Manipulators will keep exploiting until you put a stop to it. So end it now.

Chapter 6: What to Expect from Ending Manipulation

Ending manipulation is not going to be all rainbows and butterflies. Certainly, I promise you that you will reap many benefits from ending manipulation in your life. But that does not mean that the actual process will be wonderful.

Confronting a manipulator will often have your gut in knots. It can be scary, especially if a manipulator has enough of a hold on you. But that's OK. Overcoming the fear will have great results.

There will be backlash from the manipulator. He or she will not like giving up you as prey. He or she will get defensive out of self-preservation and will accuse you of making stuff up or being unreasonable. This is all just more manipulation.

You will also lose some bad friends as they realize they cannot use you anymore. But I say good riddance. You do not need these people in your life. It can be lonely at first and also painful to realize that some of your best friends are really toxic manipulators who only hung out with you to get something. But in the end, you will be glad that those people are gone.

Chapter 7: What to Do If You Are a Manipulator

Almost all self-help books and articles about manipulation are written entirely for victims. Rarely do you ever find advice for the offenders. But what if you are a manipulator? This book is different than others. We will actually help you if you are on the giving end of manipulation.

Reading this book may have made you aware of some of your own manipulative behavior. If you recognize yourself in the descriptions of how manipulators behave and what manipulative behavior entails, then you don't need to feel bad. All people employ manipulative tactics from time to time.

Sometimes, it is necessary for survival. You just need to adjust your behavior and not be manipulative as often.

But manipulation is a habit, more than anything else. You may have developed this habit in childhood, but now you cannot stop using manipulation in all of your interactions and communication. You need to realize that you do not need to manipulate people to get what you want all of the time. Sometimes, you can try just being nice and asking politely. Really, it is that simple.

Manipulation is something that you should reserve for when you really need something and cannot get it. It should not be your go-to method for dealing with others. It should also not be a weapon that you fabricate to hurt others and gain control of relationships. If you are being hurtful and constantly manipulative, you will find that the quality of your relationships leaves something to be desired. You are using people for what they have to give and not just their companionship. Therefore, you never keep friends for long. People are always getting mad at you as you cross their limits and you are always ending friendships because you do not care. You are probably very lonely. You also probably run into problems getting what you want more often than others because your manipulation backfires.

It is OK, however. You can overcome your manipulative habit. If you saw yourself in the bad parts of this book and you felt guilty, then you are obviously not a bad person. You are ready for change.

There are many psychological reasons why you may be a manipulator. It is possible that you are very lonely and have poor social skills. You may be an empath but you cannot handle your sensitivity. You may simply not have the communication skills to interact with others without employing some level of manipulation because you were raised hearing only emotional abusive and manipulative communication from your family. Or you may feel like you are not really lovable, so you thirst for control over others and seek to dominate others. Your insecurities drive you to weave traps of emotional dissonance, doubt, fear, and desire around others so that they are under your control and never abandon you.

But no matter why you are manipulative, you are acting selfishly and in a way that is hurtful to yourself as well as others. You need to find the source of your manipulative behavior and address it. This is the only that you can begin to facilitate healthy relationships that go deeper than just serving your own personal benefit.

Manipulation really is just a habit. Like all habits, you can change it into a better habit with some work. You can begin to isolate and replace your manipulative behaviors with healthier ones.

Begin working on some better communication skills, for starters. When you talk to people, work on being straightforward. You have wants and that is OK. But you don't need to treat all of your wants like some kind of covert operation. It is the adult thing to be upfront and clear about your needs, to ensure that they are met. You will be surprised at what people will do for you if you just ask nicely.

It is also important for you to begin to view people as valuable for their humanity. People are not just tools that you can use to meet your needs. They actually have a lot more to offer. People can offer you great companionship, if you take the time to appreciate them. You can find great pleasure from just getting to know people for who they are, rather than what they have to offer you.

Treat others as you would want to be treated. This golden rule is simple and relatively easy to live by. By approaching others with compassion and gentleness and not doing mean things that you would hate to have done to you, you can free yourself from a lot of problems. You will have better relationships with others as you respect their basic human rights.

You will also have a better relationship with yourself because your conscience will be clean and you will no longer feel so badly about how you treat others. In addition, you will begin to feel better about yourself as you develop more genuine relationships with people. If you act nasty, others are likely to be nasty right back to you and you will receive the same treatment that you give, but you will no longer encounter as much nastiness if you are nice to everyone. You will suffer far less. By treating others the way you want to be treated, you will find that others treat you better too. You will no longer have people treating you badly for revenge or because they do not like you and are attempting to protect themselves from your manipulative tactics. Overall, you will begin to feel better just by treating others better!

Conclusion

Whether you have been a victim or a perpetrator, you likely have experienced manipulation in your life. Almost everyone has. Most people have been manipulated and have manipulated others as they attempt to get through everyday life. Manipulation is unfortunately a major part of human communication.

But you no longer need to suffer the consequences of manipulation. Now, you have read this book and you have the power to put an end to manipulation in your life. You now know how to watch for manipulation and how to thwart the hidden agendas of manipulation. You also understand how to make yourself stronger and stop being a vulnerable target to manipulators as they scope out potential victims.

As a human being, you have certain basic rights. Manipulation violates all of those rights. It is all right for you to demand rightful and fair treatment from other people. You have the right and the power to say no to manipulators and to also confront them for their poor behavior toward you.

Do not let manipulators spin their tricks and gain control over you. Control over your life should be yours and yours alone. You do not need to give that control to anyone else. Just because someone threatens you with what scares you or offers you what you dream of, does not mean that they can actually delivery on their promises and threats. Most likely, they are only playing mind games. You can take control of your life and drop these people with only the best consequences.

It is best to no longer let others rule your life and use you. Put on end to the pain. Work on defeating manipulation today. Set boundaries and put distance from toxic people, and watch how your life begins to change.

You will find that your life is much more pleasant without crowds of toxic people leeching off of you, exploiting you for their own purposes. By demanding respect, you might enrage and even lose a lot of friends. But those friends are replaceable. You will soon find yourself attracting people who actually respect you and love you for who you are. They will be interested in knowing you, not in using you.

With more fulfilling relationships with the people in your life, your self-esteem will grow. You will also have more energy to do the things you need to do because you will not be overextending yourself emotionally and otherwise to please some manipulator in your life. You will stop feeling guilty all the time, you will no longer fear revealing your true emotions, and you will cease to doubt yourself. The benefits of demanding respect from others are boundless. They far outweigh the anger that you will be met with from the toxic people in your life when you begin to confront them.

There is no need to continue living to please others. You do not need the emotional turmoil and hurt of manipulators in your life. So why are you waiting? Start putting the tips included in these pages to use today and watch

your life transform.

Other books available by H.T. Wyatt on Kindle, paperback and audio:

No More Family Feuds: A Guide To Healing Family Wounds And Developing Stronger Family Relationships